IAN MCALLISTER & NICHOLAS READ

A BEAR'S LIFE

ORCA BOOK PUBLISHERS

Library and Archives Canada Cataloguing in Publication

McAllister, Ian, 1969-, author, photographer
A bear's life / Ian McAllister, Nicholas Read.
(My Great Bear Rainforest)

Issued in print and electronic formats.
ISBN 978-1-4598-1270-3 (hardcover).—ISBN 978-1-4598-1271-0 (pdf).—
ISBN 978-1-4598-1272-7 (epub)

1. Bears—British Columbia—Great Bear Rainforest—Juvenile literature.
2. Great Bear Rainforest (B.C.)—Juvenile literature. 3. Rain forest ecology—
British Columbia—Juvenile literature. I. Read, Nicholas, 1956—, author
II. Title.
QL737.C27M21 2017   j599.7809711'1   c2017-900776-9
                         c2017-900777-7

Summary: This nonfiction picture book is full of stunning wildlife
photographs of the bears of the Great Bear Rainforest in British Columbia.

First published in the United States, 2017
Library of Congress Control Number: 2017932493

*Orca Book Publishers is dedicated to preserving the environment and has
printed this book on Forest Stewardship Council® certified paper.*

Orca Book Publishers gratefully acknowledges the support for
its publishing programs provided by the following agencies:
the Government of Canada through the Canada Book Fund and the
Canada Council for the Arts, and the Province of British Columbia
through the BC Arts Council and the Book Publishing Tax Credit.

Cover and interior images by Ian McAllister
Edited by Sarah N. Harvey
Design by Rachel Page

About the photographs:
All of the images in this book are of wild animals in wild circumstances.
No digital manipulation or other alterations have taken place.

ORCA BOOK PUBLISHERS
www.orcabook.com

Printed and bound in Canada.

20 19 18 17 • 4 3 2 1

It's late winter in the Great Bear Rainforest.
Most bears are asleep, but not all. Some have given birth to cubs,
who will see the forest for the first time when spring arrives.

The forest has everything bears need to live
a full, rich life, but it takes a long time for cubs to learn
everything they need to know.

Adult bears are perfectly at home in the rainforest. They know that in spring there will be fresh green shoots everywhere. More than two hundred kinds of plants grow in the rainforest, and bears enjoy many of them.

A **big grizzly** has no difficulty upending a log, and a mother grizzly won't think twice about defending her cubs. But if you leave grizzlies alone, they'll leave you alone too. They'd much rather curl up for a snooze.

Cubs learn lessons from their mothers all the time, but sometimes all they want to do is play and let off steam. Just like you.

For young grizzlies, the Great Bear Rainforest is a place full of wonder and surprise. They never know what they're going to see next. A deer? A wolf? An eagle? Maybe all three.

Young grizzly bears spend a full three years
with their mothers before they strike out on their own.
Black bear cubs spend a year and a half with their
moms before going solo.

All bear cubs have to pay close attention to their mothers when they're young, because if they don't, they won't know how to survive as adults. Mother bears start teaching their young the day they leave their dens. They teach them where, when and how to find food.

They teach them what is dangerous and what is safe. In the fall they teach them to fish. Every day brings a new set of lessons for the cubs to learn. Their lives depend on it.

After male grizzlies leave their mothers, they live their whole lives alone. Females will continue to have cubs, but once males have mated, they have nothing to do with their young. They aren't social animals like people. They prefer to be by themselves.

The Great Bear Rainforest's long, jagged coastline has many rivers and streams. Bears get some of their food from these streams, especially in the fall when the salmon return. So it isn't unusual to see a bear popping out of a pool, soaking wet.

The beach can be a banquet for bears. You just have to know how to get your paws on what's there. Have you ever tried eating a barnacle? Bet you haven't. But bears are so strong they can pry them off rocks as easily as we bite corn off a cob. Then they eat them like popcorn.

They also move rocks around to set free small sea creatures like crabs, and eels, all of which make tasty bear snacks. Bears also like clams. Some bears eat just the meat inside the shell and some eat the entire clam—shell and all.

One of the most amazing sights in the Great Bear Rainforest is the spirit bear, which is a black bear born with white or cream-colored fur. The Great Bear Rainforest is the only place in the world where spirit bears live.

No one knows how many bears there are in the rainforest, but there could be thousands. And most of them are black. A black bear can have a white cub. Some mother bears have both black and white cubs. In the whole Great Bear Rainforest there are thought to be only about four hundred white bears. Some people believe that every tenth black bear is born white.

No one knows why spirit bears are white, but some scientists believe it makes them better fishers. Salmon will notice a black bear against a gray sky and move quickly to get away from it. But a white bear against the same sky might appear invisible to the fish.

Indigenous people say that Raven, the creator of the rainforest, flew among all the black bears and turned every tenth one white. This was done as a reminder of the last ice age, which ended about twelve thousand years ago. After turning the bears white, Raven promised they would be the best fishers on the coast and that they would live in peace and harmony in a forever-green rainforest.

All bears are expert fishers, but each bear has his or her own special style. Some plunge their heads into the water and grab the fish in their jaws. Others sit on the river's edge and scoop the fish up like ice cream. Some pin the salmon against the rocks with their long claws. Others jump on top of them and crush them ~~ween~~ their elbows and stomach.

Most people think bears are meat eaters, but except when they catch fish in the fall, they're mainly vegetarian. Bears love berries. And in the summer the Great Bear Rainforest is full of them. Salmonberries, devil's club berries, elderberries, twinberries, huckleberries, blueberries, thimbleberries, salal berries, gooseberries and saskatoons.

Bears eat masses of salmon because they want to fatten themselves for the long winter's sleep ahead. A sleeping bear can consume up to four thousand calories a day. That's like eating ten fish burgers. Bears' stomachs are so full and heavy when fishing season is over that they drag on the ground like sacks of grain. In fact, bears get so big they can no longer lie flat to sleep. Instead, they have to dig holes in the ground to fit their huge stomachs.

When winter comes again, bears build their dens high up in the mountains where it snows all winter long. And for a while it will look as if the Great Bear Rainforest is empty of bears. But now you know better. You know they're just having a long nap.

Also in the MY GREAT BEAR RAINFOREST series

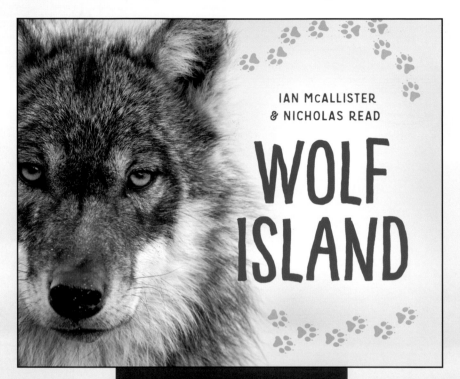

IAN McALLISTER
& NICHOLAS READ

WOLF ISLAND

9781459812642 • $ 19.95 HC • Ages 5–8

A lone wolf swims to one of the small islands that dot the rainforest's coast. The island provides him with everything he needs—deer, salmon, fresh water—everything, that is, but a mate. When a female wolf arrives on the island's rocky shores, they start a family and introduce their pups to the island's bounty.

For more of information about this spectacular place and Ian McAllister's stunning photography, please visit www.greatbearbooks.com or www.pacificwild.org.